AMISH CANNING

COOKBOOK

Delicious And Easy Homemade Recipes For

Soups, Sauces, Pickles And More

Melodi Gault

Table Of Contents

INTRODUCTION

Exploring the Rich History of Amish Canning

Amidst the idyllic landscapes and close-knit communities of the Amish, a culinary tradition as rich and heartwarming as their way of life has been passed down through generations: Amish canning. Rooted in a heritage of self-sufficiency and resourcefulness, Amish canning tells a story of preserving flavors and sustenance to bridge the gap between seasons and honor the bounties of the land.

With its origins tracing back to the 18th century, Amish canning has evolved from a means of necessity to a celebration of culture. The art of preserving was, and still is, a way for Amish families to ensure nourishment during harsh winters and cultivate a connection to the earth's cycles. The legacy of Amish canning carries a narrative of resilience, community, and profound respect for the gifts of nature.

Sarah's Story

Meet Sarah, a modern-day explorer with an insatiable curiosity for the past. Drawn to the Amish way of life, she sought a deeper connection to tradition and a respite from the fast pace of the modern world. As she delved into the world of Amish cooking, she unearthed more than just recipes – she discovered a profound way of living.

Guided by Amish culinary practices, Sarah started transforming her kitchen into a haven of simple yet nourishing creations. The act of canning became a mindful meditation, and with each jar, she captured the essence of seasons and shared the spirit of togetherness that defined the Amish community.

Sarah's pantry blossomed with colorful jams, pickles, and hearty soups, each jar a treasure trove of flavors and memories. She found herself more connected to nature, embracing the cycle of harvests and savoring the fruits of her labor throughout the year. Inspired by the Amish principles of simplicity and sustainability, Sarah not only elevated her cooking but also carved a space of tranquility in her life.

Through her journey, Sarah discovered that Amish cooking wasn't just about recipes; it was a way of infusing each meal with intention and heart. She had tapped into a rhythm that transcended time, and in doing so, found a deeper sense of fulfillment and connection that had been missing in the modern world. Sarah's story is a testament to the transformative power of embracing tradition and the joy of savoring life's simple pleasures.

Embracing the Principles of Simple, Sustainable Living

At the heart of the Amish canning tradition lies a philosophy that transcends the kitchen and touches every facet of life: simple, sustainable living. The Amish way of life is rooted in intentional choices, where every action is considered in the context of its impact on family, community, and the environment.

With their focus on using what nature provides and minimizing waste, Amish canning reflects the principles of sustainability in its purest form. Embracing locally sourced ingredients, harnessing seasonal abundance, and reusing containers are all inherent in the Amish approach to canning. It's a tribute to the belief that living in harmony with nature not only preserves the integrity of the land but also nourishes the soul.

As you journey through the pages of this cookbook, you're not just embarking on a culinary adventure but immersing yourself in a way of life that honors tradition, cherishes simplicity, and celebrates the cycles of nature. The recipes within these pages are more than just instructions; they're a testament to the enduring spirit of Amish canning, an art that speaks to the heart and sustains the body.

Join us as we uncover the secrets of Amish canning, delve into its rich history, and explore the recipes that have delighted and nourished generations. From farm-fresh vegetables to wholesome stews, each jar carries a story of resilience, love, and a commitment to the timeless values that define the Amish way of life.

ESSENTIAL CANNING TECHNIQUES AND PRACTICES

In the heart of the Amish community, canning is not merely a culinary task; it's a time-honored tradition that weaves together heritage, sustenance, and a deep appreciation for the seasons. The traditional Amish canning methods have stood the test of time, embodying a back-to-basics approach that emphasizes simplicity and practicality.

Amish canning methods draw inspiration from the past while embracing the present. From preparing homegrown produce to preserving it for future consumption, each step is infused with intention and care. The Amish have maintained practices that mirror the rhythm of nature, using techniques that encapsulate the essence of simplicity and sustainability.

Utilizing Time-Tested Canning Equipment

Just as the Amish lifestyle is characterized by simplicity, so too is their approach to canning equipment. Time-tested tools are cherished for their reliability and practicality. Envision a humble kitchen adorned with well-worn canning jars, sturdy pots, and wooden spoons – tools that have been cherished and handed down through generations.

From the iconic Mason jars to the robust canning kettles, the equipment used in Amish canning is a testament to the philosophy that function triumphs over fashion. These tools are not just utensils; they're vessels that connect generations and communities through the shared act of preservation.

Prioritizing Safety in Amish Canning Practices

While tradition is a cornerstone of Amish canning, safety takes precedence. The Amish recognize that preserving food is not only about flavor and convenience but also about nourishing their families with the utmost care. This commitment to safety is woven into every step of the process.

From meticulous cleanliness during preparation to precise processing times and pressure levels, Amish canning practices reflect an unwavering dedication to food safety. These practices have been refined over time, with each generation building on the wisdom of their predecessors.

Incorporating modern guidelines into their traditional techniques, the Amish ensure that the legacy of their canning practices remains a beacon of both flavor and security. As you engage in Amish canning, you're not just learning a skill – you're embracing a commitment to preserving wholesome and nourishing foods for your loved ones, echoing the same devotion that has guided the Amish for generations.

In the pages ahead, we'll delve deeper into the essence of Amish canning, exploring its techniques, equipment, and safety measures that infuse this culinary tradition with both heart and wisdom.

CLASSIC AMISH CANNING RECIPES

Jams, Jellies, and Fruit Preserves

1. Strawberry-Rhubarb Jam

Ingredients:
- 4 cups strawberries, hulled and chopped
- 2 cups rhubarb, diced
- 4 cups granulated sugar
- 1 packet of powdered fruit pectin

Preparation:
1. In a large pot, combine strawberries and rhubarb.
2. Mix in the powdered fruit pectin and bring the mixture to a boil over medium heat.
3. Stir in the granulated sugar and continue boiling, stirring frequently, until the mixture thickens.

4. Ladle the hot jam into sterilized jars, leaving ¼-inch headspace.

5. Wipe the jar rims, and apply sterilized lids and screw bands.

6. In a boiling water bath canner, process the jars for 10 minutes. Adjust processing time based on altitude.

2. Peach Butter

Ingredients:
- 8 cups peaches, peeled, pitted, and chopped
- 2 cups granulated sugar
- 1 teaspoon ground cinnamon
- ½ teaspoon ground nutmeg

Preparation:

1. Place the chopped peaches in a large pot and cook over medium heat until soft.

2. Use an immersion blender to puree the peaches until smooth.

3. Add sugar, cinnamon, and nutmeg to the puree, stirring well.

4. Cook the mixture over low heat, stirring frequently, until it thickens and reaches the desired consistency.

5. Ladle the peach butter into sterilized jars, leaving ½-inch headspace.

6. Remove air bubbles, wipe the jar rims, and apply sterilized lids and screw bands.

7. In a boiling water bath canner, process the jars for 15 minutes. Adjust processing time based on altitude.

3. Concord Grape Jelly

Ingredients:

- 5 cups Concord grapes, stemmed and washed
- 2 cups granulated sugar
- 1 packet of powdered fruit pectin

Preparation:

1. Crush the grapes in a large pot and bring them to a boil over medium heat.

2. Simmer for about 10 minutes, then strain the juice through a fine mesh sieve or cheesecloth.

3. Mix the grape juice and powdered fruit pectin in the pot and bring to a rolling boil.

4. Stir in the sugar and continue boiling until the mixture thickens.

5. Ladle the hot grape jelly into sterilized jars, leaving ¼-inch headspace.

6. Wipe the jar rims, and apply sterilized lids and screw bands.

7. For five minutes, process the jars in a boiling water bath canner. Adjust processing time based on altitude.

Pickles and Relishes

1. Sweet Bread and Butter Pickles

Ingredients:
- 8 cups cucumbers, sliced
- 2 cups onions, thinly sliced
- ½ cup pickling salt
- 3 cups granulated sugar
- 2 cups white vinegar
- 1 tablespoon mustard seeds

- 1 teaspoon turmeric

- ½ teaspoon of celery seeds

Preparation:

1. In a large bowl, layer cucumber and onion slices, sprinkling each layer with pickling salt. Let it sit for 2 hours.

2. Rinse the cucumber and onion slices thoroughly and drain well.

3. In a pot, combine sugar, vinegar, mustard seeds, turmeric, and celery seeds. Bring to a boil.

4. Add the cucumber and onion slices to the boiling mixture and cook for 10-15 minutes.

5. Ladle the hot pickles into sterilized jars, leaving ½-inch headspace.

6. Wipe the jar rims, and apply sterilized lids and screw bands.

7. In a boiling water bath canner, process the jars for 10 minutes. Adjust processing time based on altitude.

2. Zucchini Relish

Ingredients:

- 6 cups zucchini, grated
- 2 cups onions, finely chopped
- 2 cups red bell peppers, finely chopped
- ¼ cup pickling salt
- 3 cups granulated sugar
- 2 cups white vinegar
- 1 tablespoon mustard seeds
- 1 teaspoon turmeric
- ½ teaspoon of celery seeds

Preparation:

1. In a large bowl, combine zucchini, onions, red bell peppers, and pickling salt. Let sit for 2 hours.

2. Rinse the vegetable mixture thoroughly and drain well.

3. In a pot, combine sugar, vinegar, mustard seeds, turmeric, and celery seeds. Bring to a boil.

4. Add the vegetable mixture to the boiling mixture and cook for 10-15 minutes.

5. Ladle the hot relish into sterilized jars, leaving ½-inch headspace.

6. Wipe the jar rims, and apply sterilized lids and screw bands.

7. In a boiling water bath canner, process the jars for 15 minutes. Adjust processing time based on altitude.

3. Spicy Dill Pickles

Ingredients:
- 4 pounds pickling cucumbers
- 8 cups water
- 2 cups white vinegar
- ¼ cup pickling salt
- 4 cloves garlic, peeled
- 4 teaspoons dill seeds
- 2 teaspoons red pepper flakes

Preparation:
1. Wash and trim the ends of the cucumbers. Cut them into spears or slices as desired.

2. In a pot, combine water, vinegar, and pickling salt. Bring to a boil.

3. In each sterilized jar, place 1 clove of garlic, 1 teaspoon of dill seeds, and ½ teaspoon of red pepper flakes.

4. Pack the cucumber spears or slices into the jars tightly.

5. Ladle the hot vinegar mixture into the jars, leaving ½-inch headspace.

6. Wipe the jar rims, and apply sterilized lids and screw bands.

7. In a boiling water bath canner, process the jars for 10 minutes. Adjust processing time based on altitude.

Hearty Soups and Stews

1. The Amish version of corn soup

Ingredients:
- 4 cups cooked chicken, shredded
- 4 cups corn kernels
- 2 cups carrots, diced
- 2 cups celery, diced
- 2 cups onions, chopped
- 8 cups chicken broth
- Salt and pepper to taste

Preparation:

1. In a large pot, combine chicken, corn, carrots, celery, onions, and chicken broth.

2. Bring the mixture to a boil, then reduce the heat and simmer for about 20-25 minutes.

3. Season the soup with salt and pepper to taste.

4. Ladle the hot soup into sterilized jars, leaving 1-inch headspace.

5. Wipe the jar rims, and apply sterilized lids and screw bands.

6. Process the jars in a pressure canner at the recommended pressure for poultry dishes. Adjust processing time based on altitude.

2. Ham and Bean Stew

Ingredients:
- 4 cups cooked ham, diced
- 4 cups white beans, cooked and drained
- 2 cups carrots, diced
- 2 cups potatoes, diced
- 2 cups onions, chopped

- 8 cups ham broth or chicken broth
- Salt and pepper to taste

Preparation:

1. In a large pot, combine ham, white beans, carrots, potatoes, onions, and broth.

2. Bring the mixture to a boil, then reduce the heat and simmer for about 20-25 minutes.

3. Season the stew with salt and pepper to taste.

4. Ladle the hot stew into sterilized jars, leaving 1-inch headspace.

5. Wipe the jar rims, and apply sterilized lids and screw bands.

6. Process the jars in a pressure canner at the recommended pressure for meats. Adjust processing time based on altitude.

3. Beef and Vegetable Soup

Ingredients:

- 4 cups cooked beef, diced
- 4 cups mixed vegetables (corn, peas, carrots, green beans, etc.)

- 2 cups potatoes, diced
- 2 cups onions, chopped
- 8 cups beef broth
- Salt and pepper to taste

Preparation:

1. In a large pot, combine beef, mixed vegetables, potatoes, onions, and beef broth.

2. Bring the mixture to a boil, then reduce the heat and simmer for about 20-25 minutes.

3. Season the soup with salt and pepper to taste.

4. Ladle the hot soup into sterilized jars, leaving 1-inch headspace.

5. Wipe the jar rims, and apply sterilized lids and screw bands.

6. Process the jars in a pressure canner at the recommended pressure for meats. Adjust processing time based on altitude.

These recipes capture the essence of classic Amish canning, offering a range of flavors from sweet to savory that showcase the depth of tradition and love infused into each jar. Remember to follow proper canning practices and safety guidelines for a successful and delicious outcome.

FARM-FRESH VEGETABLES AND FRUITS

Canning Garden Bounty

1. Canned Tomatoes

Ingredients:
- Fresh tomatoes, preferably Roma or plum varieties
- Lemon juice (for acidity)

Preparation:

1. Wash and blanch the tomatoes in boiling water for about 1-2 minutes, then transfer them to an ice bath to cool.

2. Remove the tomato skins and core them.

3. Cut the tomatoes into quarters or halves, depending on size.

4. Pack the prepared tomatoes into sterilized jars, leaving ½-inch headspace.

5. Add 1 tablespoon of lemon juice to each pint jar to ensure proper acidity.

6. Wipe the jar rims, and apply sterilized lids and screw bands.

7. Process the jars in a boiling water bath canner for 40 minutes for pints and 45 minutes for quarts. Adjust processing time based on altitude.

2. Green Beans with Ham

Ingredients:

- Fresh green beans, washed and trimmed
- Cooked ham, diced
- Salt and pepper to taste

Preparation:

1. In a large pot, blanch the green beans in boiling water for about 3-4 minutes, then transfer them to an ice bath to cool.

2. In sterilized jars, layer the blanched green beans and diced ham.

3. Add salt and pepper to taste.

4. Ladle hot water or broth into the jars, leaving 1-inch headspace.

5. Wipe the jar rims, and apply sterilized lids and screw bands.

6. Process the jars in a pressure canner at the recommended pressure for meats. Adjust processing time based on altitude.

3. Spiced Apple Rings

Ingredients:
- Firm, tart apples (such as Granny Smith)
- Water
- Sugar
- Whole cloves
- Cinnamon sticks

Preparation:

1. Wash, peel, and core the apples. Cut them into rings about ½-inch thick.

2. In a pot, create a syrup by dissolving sugar in water. Add whole cloves and cinnamon sticks for flavor.

3. Bring the syrup to a boil, then reduce to a simmer.

4. Add the apple rings to the syrup and cook until they are slightly tender.

5. Pack the apple rings into sterilized jars, leaving ½-inch headspace.

6. Ladle the hot syrup over the apple rings, ensuring they are fully covered.

7. Wipe the jar rims, and apply sterilized lids and screw bands.

8. Process the jars in a boiling water bath canner for 20 minutes. Adjust processing time based on altitude.

Canning Techniques for Fruits

1. Applesauce

Ingredients:

- Apples, peeled, cored, and sliced
- Water
- Sugar (optional)
- Cinnamon (optional)

Preparation:

1. Place the sliced apples in a pot and add a small amount of water.

2. Cook the apples over medium heat until they are soft and can be easily mashed.

3. Use a potato masher or immersion blender to puree the apples into a smooth sauce.

4. Add sugar and cinnamon to taste, if desired.

5. Pack the applesauce into sterilized jars, leaving ½-inch headspace.

6. Wipe the jar rims, and apply sterilized lids and screw bands.

7. Process the jars in a boiling water bath canner for 20 minutes. Adjust processing time based on altitude.

2. Canned Peaches in Light Syrup

Ingredients:
- Fresh peaches, peeled, pitted, and sliced
- Water
- Sugar

Preparation:

1. In a pot, create a light syrup by dissolving sugar in water. Use approximately 2 cups of sugar for every 4 cups of water.

2. Bring the syrup to a boil, then reduce to a simmer.

3. Add the peach slices to the syrup and blanch them for about 1-2 minutes.

4. Pack the blanched peach slices into sterilized jars, leaving ½-inch headspace.

5. Ladle the hot syrup over the peaches, ensuring they are fully covered.

6. Wipe the jar rims, and apply sterilized lids and screw bands.

7. Process the jars in a boiling water bath canner for 20 minutes. Adjust processing time based on altitude.

3. Pear Preserves

Ingredients:

- Firm, ripe pears, peeled, cored, and sliced
- Lemon juice
- Sugar
- Ground ginger
- Ground cinnamon

Preparation:

1. In a pot, create a syrup by dissolving sugar in water. Use approximately 2 cups of sugar for every 4 cups of water.

2. Add ground ginger and ground cinnamon to the syrup for flavor.

3. Bring the syrup to a boil, then reduce to a simmer.

4. Add the pear slices to the syrup and blanch them for about 1-2 minutes.

5. Pack the blanched pear slices into sterilized jars, leaving ½-inch headspace.

6. Add 1 tablespoon of lemon juice to each pint jar to prevent browning.

7. Ladle the hot syrup over the pears, ensuring they are fully covered.

8. Wipe the jar rims, and apply sterilized lids and screw bands.

9. Process the jars in a boiling water bath canner for 20 minutes. Adjust processing time based on altitude.

These recipes celebrate the vibrant flavors of farm-fresh vegetables and fruits, showcasing the art of preserving nature's bounty in every jar. With careful preparation and adherence to canning safety, these preserves will bring the taste of the harvest season to your table throughout the year.

AMISH FLAVORS: RELISHING TRADITION

Crafting Homemade Salsas

1. Tomato-Corn Salsa

Ingredients:
- 4 cups tomatoes, diced
- 2 cups corn kernels (fresh, frozen, or canned)
- 1 cup onions, chopped
- ½ cup green bell pepper, chopped
- ½ cup red bell pepper, chopped
- ¼ cup jalapeno pepper, minced (adjust for desired heat)
- 3 cloves garlic, minced
- ¼ cup fresh cilantro, chopped
- ½ cup white vinegar
- 1 teaspoon salt
- 1 teaspoon cumin

- ½ teaspoon of black pepper

Preparation:

1. In a large pot, combine tomatoes, corn, onions, bell peppers, jalapeno peppers, and garlic.

2. Add vinegar, salt, cumin, and black pepper. Mix well.

3. Bring the mixture to a boil and simmer for about 10 minutes, stirring occasionally.

4. Stir in the cilantro and cook for an additional 2 minutes.

5. Ladle the hot salsa into sterilized jars, leaving ½-inch headspace.

6. Wipe the jar rims, and apply sterilized lids and screw bands.

7. In a boiling water bath canner, process the jars for 15 minutes. Adjust processing time based on altitude.

2. Sweet and Spicy Peach Salsa

Ingredients:

- 4 cups peaches, peeled, pitted, and diced
- 1 cup onions, chopped

- ¼ cup jalapeno pepper, minced (adjust for desired heat)
- ¼ cup red bell pepper, chopped
- 1 cup white vinegar
- ½ cup granulated sugar
- 1 teaspoon ground cumin
- ½ teaspoon ground cinnamon
- ¼ teaspoon cayenne pepper

Preparation:

1. In a large pot, combine peaches, onions, jalapeno peppers, and red bell peppers.

2. Add vinegar, sugar, cumin, cinnamon, and cayenne pepper. Mix well.

3. Bring the mixture to a boil and simmer for about 10 minutes, stirring occasionally.

4. Ladle the hot salsa into sterilized jars, leaving ½-inch headspace.

5. Wipe the jar rims, and apply sterilized lids and screw bands.

6. In a boiling water bath canner, process the jars for 15 minutes. Adjust processing time based on altitude.

Chutneys and Condiments

1. Apple-Raisin Chutney

Ingredients:
- 6 cups apples, peeled, cored, and chopped
- 1 cup onions, chopped
- 1 cup golden raisins
- 2 cups brown sugar
- 2 cups white vinegar
- 1 teaspoon ground ginger
- ½ teaspoon ground cinnamon
- ¼ teaspoon ground cloves

Preparation:

1. In a large pot, combine apples, onions, and golden raisins.

2. Add brown sugar, white vinegar, ground ginger, ground cinnamon, and ground cloves.

3. Bring the mixture to a boil and simmer for about 30-40 minutes, stirring occasionally.

4. Ladle the hot chutney into sterilized jars, leaving ½-inch headspace.

5. Wipe the jar rims, and apply sterilized lids and screw bands.

6. Process the jars in a boiling water bath canner for 20 minutes. Adjust processing time based on altitude.

2. Pickled Red Beets

Ingredients:
- Fresh red beets, peeled and sliced
- 2 cups white vinegar
- 1 cup water
- 1 cup granulated sugar
- 1 teaspoon whole cloves
- 1 teaspoon mustard seeds

Preparation:
1. In a pot, combine white vinegar, water, sugar, whole cloves, and mustard seeds.

2. Bring the mixture to a boil, then reduce to a simmer.

3. In sterilized jars, pack the sliced beets tightly.

4. Pour the hot pickling liquid over the beets, ensuring they are fully covered.

5. Wipe the jar rims, and apply sterilized lids and screw bands.

6. Process the jars in a boiling water bath canner for 30 minutes. Adjust processing time based on altitude.

These recipes capture the essence of Amish flavors, offering a delightful array of salsas, chutneys, and condiments that elevate any meal. As you savor these recipes, you're not just indulging in delectable tastes, but immersing yourself in the cherished traditions that have graced Amish tables for generations.

HOMEMADE COMFORT: AMISH CANNED COMFORT FOODS

Canning Meats and Poultry

1. Canned Beef Stew

Ingredients:
- 4 cups beef, cubed
- 4 cups potatoes, diced
- 2 cups carrots, diced
- 2 cups onions, chopped
- 2 cups celery, diced
- 4 cups beef broth
- Salt and pepper to taste

Preparation:
1. In a large pot, brown the cubed beef over medium heat until evenly seared.

2. Add potatoes, carrots, onions, and celery to the pot.

3. Pour in beef broth andand season with salt and pepper.

4. Bring the mixture to a boil, then reduce to a simmer and cook until the vegetables are tender.

5. Ladle the hot beef stew into sterilized jars, leaving 1-inch headspace.

6. Wipe the jar rims, and apply sterilized lids and screw bands.

7. Process the jars in a pressure canner at the recommended pressure for meats. Adjust processing time based on altitude.

2. Amish Pork and Beans

Ingredients:

- 4 cups cooked pork, shredded
- 4 cups cooked white beans
- 2 cups tomato sauce
- 1 cup brown sugar
- 1 tablespoon mustard
- 1 teaspoon salt

- 1 teaspoon black pepper

Preparation:

1. In a pot, combine cooked pork, white beans, tomato sauce, brown sugar, mustard, salt, and black pepper.

2. Bring the mixture to a simmer and cook for about 15-20 minutes, stirring occasionally.

3. Ladle the hot pork and beans into sterilized jars, leaving 1-inch headspace.

4. Wipe the jar rims, apply sterilized lids, and screw bands.

5. Process the jars in a pressure canner at the recommended pressure for meats. Adjust processing time based on altitude.

Filling Pantry with Delightful Desserts

1. Spiced Apple Pie Filling

Ingredients:

- 8 cups apples, peeled, cored, and sliced
- 2 cups granulated sugar
- ½ cup cornstarch
- 1 teaspoon ground cinnamon
- ¼ teaspoon ground nutmeg
- ¼ teaspoon of ground cloves
- 4 cups water
- ½ cup lemon juice

Preparation:

1. In a pot, create a syrup by dissolving sugar in water.

2. Add cornstarch, ground cinnamon, ground nutmeg, and ground cloves to the syrup. Mix well.

3. Bring the mixture to a boil and cook until thickened.

4. Stir in lemon juice and add sliced apples to the pot. Cook for about 5 minutes.

5. Ladle the hot spiced apple pie filling into sterilized jars, leaving ½-inch headspace.

6. Wipe the jar rims, and apply sterilized lids and screw bands.

7. Process the jars in a boiling water bath canner for 20 minutes. Adjust processing time based on altitude.

2. Cherry Pie Filling

Ingredients:
- 8 cups cherries, pitted
- 2 cups granulated sugar
- ½ cup cornstarch
- 1 teaspoon almond extract
- 4 cups water
- ½ cup lemon juice

Preparation:
1. In a pot, create a syrup by dissolving sugar in water.

2. Add cornstarch to the syrup and mix well.

3. Bring the mixture to a boil and cook until thickened.

4. Stir in almond extract and lemon juice.

5. Add pitted cherries to the pot and cook for about 5 minutes.

6. Ladle the hot cherry pie filling into sterilized jars, leaving ½-inch headspace.

7. Wipe the jar rims, and apply sterilized lids and screw bands.

8. Process the jars in a boiling water bath canner for 20 minutes. Adjust processing time based on altitude.

These recipes bring the heartwarming flavors of Amish comfort to your pantry, offering nourishing dishes and delectable desserts that will surely warm your soul. As you savor these canned creations, you're not just indulging in comforting fare – you're embracing the essence of Amish tradition and the joy of sharing homemade delights with your loved ones.

PRESERVING AMISH TRADITIONS: BEYOND CANNING

Cultivating an Amish-Inspired Pantry

Cultivating an Amish-inspired pantry goes beyond the act of canning; it's about curating a collection of wholesome ingredients that echo the simplicity and sustenance of Amish living. With a well-stocked pantry, you can effortlessly recreate the flavors of traditional Amish meals year-round. Start by ensuring you have a variety of canned goods, including jams, jellies, fruits, vegetables, and soups, that reflect the essence of your canning journey. Add to this a selection of dried herbs, spices, flours, grains, and other staples that form the foundation of Amish cuisine.

Incorporating Canned Goods into Traditional Recipes

Amish cooking is known for its humble yet robust flavors, and the inclusion of canned goods can take these traditional recipes to new heights. Think about adding a dollop of spiced apple pie filling to your morning oatmeal, or using canned tomatoes to create a rich and hearty tomato sauce for pasta. Incorporating canned goods into classic recipes not only adds convenience but also preserves the genuine flavors of Amish traditions. Whether it's a jar of pickled beets in your salad or canned peaches in light syrup for dessert, these ingredients connect you with the heritage of Amish cooking.

Craft Ideas for Preserving and Gifting Canned Delights

Preserving the flavors of Amish traditions extends beyond the kitchen and into thoughtful craft projects.

As you create a beautiful array of canned goods, consider ways to present them as heartfelt gifts or charming home decor. Tie a ribbon around a jar of homemade jam and pair it with a fresh loaf of bread for a welcoming gift. Craft personalized labels for your canned creations, showcasing your dedication to preserving Amish flavors. Additionally, you can assemble charming gift baskets with an assortment of canned goods, along with recipe cards that invite others to share in the joy of Amish cooking.

By embracing the art of cultivating a pantry, incorporating canned delights into recipes, and infusing your creations with the spirit of craftsmanship, you're not only preserving Amish traditions but also sharing a piece of their cherished culture with those around you. These practices celebrate the time-honored values of simplicity, community, and the joy of sharing nourishing food with loved ones.

MODERN APPLICATIONS OF AMISH CANNING

Adapting Amish Canning Practices for Contemporary Kitchens

In a world driven by technological advancements, the timeless art of Amish canning finds its place in modern kitchens by seamlessly integrating tradition with innovation. Adapting these practices means embracing the essence of Amish preservation while utilizing modern tools and resources. Today's pressure canners, water bath canners, and reliable thermometers enhance safety and precision, ensuring your canning endeavors are both effective and efficient. With access to informative resources and recipes online, you can master Amish canning techniques regardless of your background.

Incorporating Sustainability and Simplicity into Modern Living

Amish canning isn't just about preserving flavors; it's a way of life that champions sustainability and simplicity. As modern living becomes increasingly fast-paced, the principles of Amish canning offer a counterbalance. By growing your own produce or sourcing from local farms, you reduce food miles and support sustainable agriculture. Canning empowers you to enjoy seasonal flavors year-round, reducing the need for excessive packaging and preserving the nutritional value of your food. Moreover, adopting these practices encourages a return to mindful consumption and a connection to the source of your sustenance.

By embracing the adaptability of Amish canning methods and weaving them into the fabric of modern living, you not only enjoy the rewards of preserving nature's bounty but also contribute to a more sustainable, intentional, and nourishing way of life.

COOKING AND SAVORING AMISH CREATIONS

Unleashing the Flavors of Preserved Foods in Amish Recipes

Cooking and savoring Amish creations isn't just about opening a jar – it's about unearthing a world of flavors meticulously preserved in each container. As you incorporate canned goods into Amish recipes, you're not just adding ingredients; you're infusing every dish with the history, love, and tradition that come with Amish canning. Imagine the velvety texture of spiced apple pie filling enveloped in a flaky crust or the rich aroma of tomato-corn salsa mingling with freshly grilled meats. These preserved treasures serve as the foundation for wholesome, flavorful meals that effortlessly pay homage to Amish culinary heritage.

Sharing Meals and Traditions with Family and Friends

The act of cooking and sharing Amish creations goes beyond the plate – it's a heartfelt experience that binds generations and creates lasting memories. Gathered around a table laden with nourishing dishes, you share not only the food but the stories, values, and traditions of the Amish way of life. The aroma of a simmering beef stew or the sweetness of peach pie filling invokes a sense of togetherness, inviting loved ones to partake in the warmth of your kitchen and the beauty of Amish culture. Through these shared meals, you strengthen family bonds and forge connections that transcend time and distance.

Cooking and savoring Amish creations is more than a culinary endeavor; it's a profound journey into the heart of tradition, community, and the joy of gathering. As you explore the depths of flavor that Amish canning brings to your table, you're not only nourishing your body but also nourishing your soul and the spirits of those who join you in savoring these treasured dishes.

CONCLUSION

In the heartwarming pages of this book, you've embarked on a journey through time, tradition, and taste – a journey that delves deep into the cherished world of Amish canning. As you've explored the meticulous techniques, heartfelt recipes, and rich history of preserving, you've not only gained the skills to can and store nature's bounty but also cultivated a profound appreciation for the time-honored Amish way of life. In reflecting on the timeless art of Amish canning, you've rekindled a connection to heritage, simplicity, and the joy of savoring the fruits of your labor.

As you stand at the crossroads of tradition and modernity, your journey into the world of Amish canning wouldn't be complete without extending heartfelt gratitude to the Amish culinary legacy. This legacy – steeped in community, sustainability, and unwavering values – has generously shared its secrets, allowing you to become a steward of time-tested techniques and flavors. With each jar you seal, each recipe you master, and each meal you share, you honor the Amish heritage that has illuminated your culinary path.

With newfound skills and a heart enriched by Amish values, you're now equipped to embrace the art of canning with a profound sense of purpose. As you bring forth the flavors, memories, and traditions that this journey has bestowed upon you, you're not only preserving food but weaving the threads of a cherished heritage into the fabric of your own life. So, go forth, unleash your creativity, and preserve not just nature's bounty, but the beauty of Amish culture itself.

Thank you for embarking on this enriching journey with us. Your dedication to preserving tradition and embracing the timeless art of Amish canning fills us with warmth and gratitude.

Happy canning and savoring!

Made in United States
Orlando, FL
21 September 2024

51756773R00036